DEEP STATE DEFECTOR V

DEEP STATE DEFECTOR V

Rahul Manchanda

To order additional copies of this book, contact:
Xlibris
844-714-8691
www.Xlibris.com
Orders@Xlibris.com
849946

CONTENTS

CHAPTER 1

The Seedy And Unregulated World Of Underwiters And Risk Departments In The Financial Industry

There is no more seedier and sinister underworld than the realm of the Financial Company "Underwriter" or "Risk Analysis Department."

These entities are akin to the Big Tech knee-jerk response of the "all-powerful algorithm" whenever someone calls out a search engine like Google or business review site like Yelp for being biased, racist, discriminatory, corrupt, or in any other way exerting way too much influence where they should not be.

That is why there is little to no wonder that these 2 departments are usually shrouded in complete and total secrecy, where you can't even find out the names of the people that arbitrarily attacked you, denied you credit, a mortgage, closed your bank account, canceled your account, or any other action designed to sabotage your life, your family, or your business.

And it's also no wonder that it is also used by the corrupted global Oligarchs to destroy and legally and equitably assassinate any of their targets in the arenas described above.

If one performs a search online, looking to find some type of law enforcement agency (or even ethics group) which could open up a *bona fide*, legitimate inquiry into the inner workings and decision making process of these "underwriters," one comes up empty handed, again and again.

That's because, just like with the unseemly word of employment "headhunters," there is none, because it is also primarily a tool of the super wealthy global oligarchy to dismantle, destroy, keep down, and ruin their targets and/or whomever that they perceive to be the "peasant class."

The global oligarchs have hoarded away all of the world's money, tangible assets, gold, jewelry, real estate, diamonds, precious metals, and other physical forms of wealth, while refusing to share it or even loan it at decent interest rates, to those that they hate or want to suffer.

Consequently, if your political opinions, or religious convictions, or even your own morals and ethics clash and conflict with said Oligarchy, your life will be guaranteed to be constantly attacked and sabotaged, with no help or lifelines from any financial company, or law enforcement agency, as a result, thus dooming you, your family, and your business to poverty, failure, obscurity, and extinction.

That's why the world of the underwriter (see, undertaker) is more akin to legal and equitable assassination squads, or as the Israeli Mossad likes to call them the *"Kidon,"* in order to wipe out the enemies or obstructions of complete and total global oligarchical and unrivaled control of the planet that we all share and live on.

U.S. Senators Bernie Sanders and Elizabeth Warren, who often crow on about the "oligarchs" and the "billionaire class," for some reason never address or discuss the cursed "underwriters" or "risk departments" of any of these massive financial institutions (banks, merchant services, credit card companies, mortgages, insurance, real estate) because they know that their campaign election checks and "donations" would quickly go the way of the "do do bird" to extinction and dry up faster than shit goes through a goose.

It is the words that you never utter, or try to regulate (or legislate) if you are one of the many hypocritical cowards inhabiting the United States government, in any one of the 3 branches executive, legislative and judiciary.

Mahatma Gandhi once said, "hate the sin, love the sinner," but with underwriters and risk departments of financial institutions, it is impossible to know the difference, because they are kept far more secretive and out of the light of law and scrutiny than any other secret society hitherto described, with infinite more power to destroy and target at will, with little to zero appeal process or due process rights afforded to their victims.

To that end, if you are an individual or small business owner (non-Oligarch) who enjoys and appreciates, freedom, self-sufficiency, fair dealing, hard work, honesty, a level playing field, a fair days pay for a fair days work, or any of the other hackneyed phrases indicating your healthy respect for law and order, then you will immediately pick up your phone or your laptop and contact your local congressman or senator and tell them to immediately begin an investigation into the seedy underworld of the "underwriter" and the "risk department" phenomenon of every single financial institution that exists on planet earth.

And then watch as the grass once again turns green, the skies turn bright blue, and the money starts to flow again to the people and places that need it the most, and not into the coffers of the corrupt, bloated, sick, perverted, and deviant members of the Oligarchical Class, so that they alone can buy the latest Ferraris and Bugattis with **_YOUR_** money.

CHAPTER 2

The War In Ukraine Is Ground Zero For The New World Orders Human Values

It doesn't take a genius to quickly deduce that the war in Ukraine by and between the Russian Federation and the United States (NATO) is literally Ground ZERO for the ultimate and final war pertaining to what exactly will be the final version and universal acceptance of our human values, as a global civilization.

The rhetoric that is being thrown around (by each side, many of whom have been dishonestly silenced/censored/drowned out by others) makes it clear that there are many salient but fundamental human values at odds with one another throughout the world, that can no longer be ironed or hammered out in our global international universities, conferences, meetings, even the internet and social media where these human values are bandied about, shot down or propped up, by whomever and whatever these citizens of the world believe.

Indeed, some of these nations, the ones blessed with more cash, weapons, GDP, global reach, and aggressive statesmen, have pushed the narrative that anyone opposing their value systems, are somehow "terrorists" or "upstarts," which ironically, is as old as civilization itself.

The ancient Romans used to call the relatively hairy, dirty, brambly, and wooly Britons to their North (today's modern day United Kingdom) as well as the supposedly uncivilized, blood thirsty, traitorous Visigoths towards their East (today's Germany and Slovaks) the "Barbarus," or barbarians, much like our United States Department of State calls today's versions of those people who refuse to submit or conform to their will, as "terrorists."

It is well known that de-humanizing ones' enemies is the quickest most effective way to galvanize the masses to fight one another at the behest of their oligarch leaders who have always, completely purchased and bought off its politicians and government.

So it is actually quite the misguided view to assume that this war is simply about the plot of land lying by and between the Russian Federation and Poland/Germany, the Ukraine, but rather, a global war which is also being fought in the highest courts of the United States, in the international media, in our official sanctions and financial blockade policies, in our congressional and senatorial legislation for example pertaining to gun control, within big technology grappling with the limits of freedom of speech and/or incitement to violence, and so many more arenas that are certainly not confined or constrained to Ukraine proper.

Undersigned author has made note of several different types of value systems that are currently being debated through war now, with Ukraine representing the United States and the West with NATO, as against the Russian Federation with allies rooted in the deeply religious and moral halls of Orthodox Christianity and Islam, as well as traditional patriarchal societies in Eurasia, Africa, South America and Asia.

Issues being fought on the battlefield include, but are not limited to:

(1) abortion on demand,

(2) extreme homosexual rights (or existence),

(3) extreme feminism,

(4) the rights of children,

(5) extreme jewish zionism,

(6) extreme minority rights to the point of usurping their countries' majority populations,

(7)   immigration and emigration,

(8)   irresponsible wars with no proof/evidence/probable cause,

(9)   proxy wars used by bigger more powerful nations,

(10) oil and gas rights,

(11) water rights,

(12) ethnic cleansing,

(13) cultural superiority,

(14) cultural inferiority,

(15) modes of human governance such as communism, capitalism, theocracy, fascism, socialism,

(16) border integrity versus open societies,

(17) racial superiority versus racial inferiority, and

(18) scores of other issues.

When one understands that these are, for example, some of the many issues being fought over right now within battlefield ground zero being the Ukraine, without taking into account either your own citizenship or country of residence, or your opponent's, one finds that you may have more in common with the country(s) that your own country(s) are fighting.

This is the first time in history that this has occurred on such a grand global scale, a battle for human values, because the victor today, will lead the groundwork and pathway permanently for the global society to trod down, into eternity.

And that's why everyone has a stake in what is happening in the war in the Ukraine.

CHAPTER 3

The Weaponization Of Employment Headhunters By The Global Oligarchs

Apparently, one of the only industries left in the United States of America that has been left unregulated, not even codified in ethics principles, is the perfidious and sullied world of Employment Headhunters.

Often confused with their more civilized cousin, Employment Recruiters, Employment Headhunters, hitherto "Headhunters," are literally staffed by some of the most unsavory, unethical, dishonest, scurrilous, sociopathic, mercenary, money hungry, and devoid of any decency individuals who are often weaponized by their mainly wealthy, oligarchy based clientele, simply for the fact that no one in their right mind could, or would, pay anyone up to 50% of the annual salary of a prospective employee up front, unless they either (1) knew that the prospective employee would generate 1000-fold in profits, or (2) wanted to sabotage or destroy another entity's (usually a competitor) business.

And this may the main reason that the world of Headhunters is unregulated - because only the super wealthy need apply.

In some ways, Headhunters are akin to underworld sins and crimes, such as illegal narcotics, sexual deviancy, weapons of mass destruction trafficking, high class prostitution, assassination, and other arenas too creepy to be described here.

But as a very famous international business magnate once said, "Everything is for sale, if the price is right."

How fitting that this quote came from a super wealthy international business man.

Nowadays, all an oligarch-run company has to do, to upset the apple cart in any well-run company, is to hire a Headhunter to tempt and then steal that company's most prized employee(s), and this will in turn quickly bring the targeted company (and its CEO) to existential, financial, and logistical ruin.

The thieving oligarch company often then cynically turns around and fires that stolen employee, discarding them after only a few weeks/months, just long enough after the trust and good will has been completely destroyed by and between the former company and their prized employee.

The only other methods to do that are clearly illegal, if not unethical - such as the methods described above.

So why then, has no one in the United States government either organized or targeted the Headhunter industry for legal regulation, reporting requirements, rules and guidelines, or even ethics?

Even journalism has these types of codes.

Well, as was indicated above, just as the super wealthy generally do not believe that the law or ethics applies to them, similarly the weaponization of the Headhunter is also an unregulated weapon in their arsenal of unfair competition and deceptive business practices.

Hopefully the three branches of government will begin to take notice of this nefarious field of endeavor, and begin to get involved so that young, green, start up companies will also have a chance to flourish and grow, without having their wings periodically clipped (if not de-fanged) by the bullying oligarchs that are already established in their chosen field.

Chapter 4

International Communism Latest Stunt Creating A Problem And Then Introducing The Solution – Increased Crime In The Inner Cities

In the latest display of the age old International Communist strategy of "Create the Problem, And Then Introduce The (Communist Draconian) Solution," New York City is the prime example of this mechanism on full display.

Right now the pivotal important members of the United States Government within New York City are either fully Communist or tools of Communism, wherein they are either contributing to or allowing a massive increase of scary, violent, life threatening, debilitating crime to take over, without any consequences to those criminals by a relatively lax and non-caring District Attorney Alvin Bragg, under the guise of "racial justice" and "reversing discrimination," since the vast majority of those arrested and incarcerated in the past few decades have been minority and black Americans.

However, just like the same justice infrastructure currently existing in Los Angeles and New Orleans, Communists require the "informed consent", or rather, the "manufactured consent," of the "People" in order to usher itself in, and this time they are hoping, with another introduction of the draconian "Violent Crime Control Law Enforcement Act of 1994," aka the "1994 Crime Bill," which was both drafted and passed by then President Bill Clinton and then Senator Joe Biden, the latter of whom is now, obviously, President Joe Biden.

That horrific 1994 Crime Bill incarcerated not only criminals (which is good) but also grabbed within their net, tens of millions of innocent minorities and black Americans, and gave too much power to the local (and often documented racist) police departments of America, and provided 100,000 new officers per state, to drag the United States kicking and screaming towards a full fledged Police State, wherein 1/3 of all blacks were incarcerated, 1/6 of all latinos were incarcerated, and 1/5 of all poor whites were incarcerated, and given criminal records.

70 million Americans (1/3 of all adults) were given a criminal record because of Joe Biden and Bill Clinton, and that is more than the population of France.

This is clearly not an ideal solution.

How about a more moderate approach to dealing with and solving this artificial increase in violent crime, and learning from America's past?

How about merging what we have learned, not repeating the sins of the past, before we implement new draconian crime control bills that are coming down the pike?

Republican Senator Marsha Blackburn is now apparently the "chosen one," tweeting on and on about cleaning up crime, introducing new legislation to aggressively combat violent crime, etc, so much so that it recalls Shakespeare's Hamlet wherein "The Lady Doth Protest Too Much."

In that play, Queen Gertrude utters that phrase in response to the insincere overacting of a character in the play within a play created by Prince Hamlet to prove his uncle's guilt in the murder of his father, the King of Denmark.

This phrase is used in everyday speech to indicate doubt of someone's sincerity, especially regarding the truth of a strong denial.

This phenomenon is emblematic of International Communism's complete and total mastery of "Reaction Formation," where in psychoanalytic theory, reaction formation (German: Reaktionsbildung) is a defense mechanism in which emotions and impulses which are anxiety-producing or perceived to be unacceptable are mastered by exaggeration of the directly opposing tendency.

In other words, "create the problem, introduce the (Communist) solution."

So be aware and be careful of International Communism's next "solution" coming down the pike, and just like in the movie The Godfather, when then Vito Corleone tells his son Michael Corleone, that "whoever comes to you with this Barzini meeting, that's the traitor."

Similarly, the next U.S. Government puppet or monied Non-Governmental Organization ("NGO") lackey that introduces the latest draconian crime bill, will be the new and next Communist traitor to the American people's freedom, constitutional rights, and civil liberties.

And remember, International Communists care little to nothing about "political affiliation" or "political party," so since the Democrats in the USA have already been firmly labeled to be "leftist socialist communist pinkos" by the American people, the traitor will most likely come as a thief in the night, in Republican form (see above Republican U.S. Senator Marsha Blackburn, for example).

Maybe somebody should look into her latest political campaign donations, and their communist sources.

CHAPTER 5

The Consumer Financial Protection Bureau and NYS Department of Financial Services Are Inherently Useless, And Probably Harmful To Financial Company Consumers

There was once upon a time, when customers of a bank, insurance company, debt collector, or even a ruthless mortgage company, could file a scathing complaint which would land directly square on the proverbial chin of the bank and its corporate betters, simply by writing a letter, making a phone call, or emailing their customer service department.

At that point in time, the customer had successfully targeted and connected with the bank personnel, who upon receiving said complaint, would immediately snap into action, become introspective, and worst case scenario, hand it off to their lawyers to respond to.

But at least, these financial institutions' "betters" would **_READ_** the complaint, and therefore internalize it to some extent.

Now however, with the advent of the Consumer Financial Protection Bureau ("CFPB"), and its little bastard brother, the New York State Department of Finance ("NYSDFS"), complaints, which have now become far more frequent due to the cycle of abuse described below, rarely if ever reach the financial institutions' "betters," and therefore rarely, if ever, have their intended effect of resolution, improvement, or conciliation of the customer's woes.

That's because greedy, sociopathic, blood sucker, catatonic lawyers have insulated the complaint process from soup to nuts, A to Z, after they have left the complainant's fingertips.

Even the agencies described above, CFPB and NYS DFS, take in the complaint with little to no human involvement, assign it a random docket number to give the customer a false sense of security or accomplishment, but then immediately shunt it off, without doing any provable research or investigation, on to the targeted financial institution itself, whereby it is met by another machine-like process, shunted into the ever growing but never resolved "pile of complaints," where it is then divided like a stack of playing cards to its ever growing roster of customer service monkeys who color and key code their "responses" by pressing buttons all day, with the end goal being at best, case dismissal, and at least, simply a message conveyed by the CFPB and/or NYSDFS that the "company has responded, and therefore the complaint is closed" bullshit outcome.

At no time or point in this process does any financial employee "better" see, read, or review the complaint, let alone take it to heart to improve their institution, because they simple do not have to do so.

And even if they wanted to do so, and had the best of intentions, they are prevented by the seemingly airtight corruption/preordained complaint dismissal process already baked into this system.

The end result is that the CFPB and NYSDFS, while already getting mercilessly attacked by the Republican congressional and senatorial prostitutes sucking at the teet of big banks, big insurance, big real estate, and big merchant services, are anyway reduced to full neuter-dom by their own stupid and redundant actions described above.

In fact, one could argue that no better shield to big finance has emerged than these 2 cursed agencies, who by and large keep problems under lock and key, never to see the sun, and never to be exposed.

And therein lies the rub.

Chapter 6

Google's Public Foes Exist Merely To Fool The Public

Over the past decade, since this issue came to a head, there have been several very prominent politicians, senators, congressmen, executive level bureaucrats, business owners, celebrities, media personalities, judges, and even talk show hosts both in the United States and overseas, who have complained bitterly that the Google search engine is all at once corrupt, does not distribute search results in line with neutral "algorithms," and is by and large controlled by a few number of truly evil people that have selected a few thousand other evil people, to control the news and information out there not just for Americans, but for the entire world.

If one reads between the lines, the reason that nothing negative has happened to Google, such as what would first come to mind, i.e., antitrust or monopoly breakup, criminal investigations and exposure of the very souls at Google who have created this fundamentally corrupt paradigm, or indictment for public corruption the various government actors whose charge it was to bring Google down and/or expose their criminality, we see that it is in fact the awesome money power (some would call it bribery, and some would call it lobbying) that Google spreads around to all sides, the Democrats, the Republicans, Green Party, Communists, Socialists, and everyone else in between, because Google is wildly successful at convincing any of its main critics that it is not only serving their interests, but "here, take this briefcase of money for your day to day needs."

Obviously the latter act is usually the most convincing.

But really let's call it out for what it is - bribery and corruption.

But it would not be so serious as it is now, getting to the bottom of the proverbial ninth inning, with bases loaded, if we did not also now have wars breaking out all over the world, in the Ukraine, in Hong Kong, South China Sea, India and Pakistan, and other hot spots where the end result is most certainly global nuclear annihilation.

And Google, certainly has "picked sides."

In fact, the United States government, through various whore-like mouthpieces, has actually defended Google's unchecked growth and dangerous filtration of the information out there with weak sauce phrases like "we don't want to destroy our own tech giant so that China takes its place," or "Big Tech dominated by America is always a strength," and other such nonsense, since Google does not serve America, but rather its own corporate board and its shareholders.

In fact Google used to always be in the world wide news for being taken down by one country or another, sometimes in Russia, sometimes in France, or perhaps maybe Spain, or generally in the European Union, for high crimes and misdemeanors such as massive tax evasion and violations, antitrust activity, illegal election interference, incitement to violence in ethnic tension hot spots, aiding and abetting color revolutions all of the world led by megalomaniacs such as George Soros, search engine manipulation to favor one product over another, or one politician over another, one religion or culture over another, or one form of government over another.

But for some reason, all of that great "Google News" has all but evaporated, while its enemies who used to report its wrongdoings have lost their broadcasting licenses by actual governments or have been search engine de-listed, jailed, arrested, incarcerated, blocked or banned by Google and its affiliates to protect itself and its criminal employees.

And so once again, we return to who exactly have been the major players over the past decade that have destroyed or weakened these efforts to bring Google to task over their violations?

Well unfortunately many of those individuals who once (and still do) promised to bring Google to its knees and/or break them up or reform them (and had the power to do so) were probably either "lobbied to stop," bought out, threatened, replaced, silenced or whatever, or maybe they just know how to bullshit the American people really very well.

So lets list some of them, shall we?

U.S. Senator Josh Hawley, FTC Chair Lina Khan, former Department of Justice Antitrust Division Chief Makan Delrahim, former Google evil doers Eric Schmidt and Jared Cohen, current Google CEO and chosen fall-guy Sundar Pichai, Google original founders Larry Page and Sergey Brin, former FTC Antitrust Chairwoman Edith Ramirez, Jonathan Kanter current DOJ Antitrust Division Chief, former Google Legal Counsel Kent Walker, current Google Counsel Halimah DeLaine Prado, and even current federal judge Amit Mehta who is presiding over the latest federal government' weak-kneed court attempt to bring Google to heel, and scores of other culprits.

CHAPTER 7

For Global Peace, It Is Incumbent Upon Saudi Arabia And Israel To Share Wealth And Power With Iran

The ancient historical battle by and between the rich monarchies and their vassals has always driven history, according to Karl Marx who derived his views in part from the philosophy of G.W.F. Hegel, who conceived of history as the dialectical self-development of "spirit."

In the current situation, although Iran can hardly be considered a vassal state, its values are clearly aligned with the meek and the poor throughout the Middle East, and with the oppressed.

This is why they have thrown their lot in with the Palestinians, who fight and resist the Israelis who can be considered an extension of European (and now American) colonial power and wealth, backed up by millennia of plunder and war and amassed gold from all of the corners of the world.

Therefore Iran should be respected as the proverbial "underdog" fighting against the rich bullies of the Middle East, Saudi Arabia, Europe, United States, Great Britain, and Israel.

The Founding Fathers would have sympathized with this geopolitical position, as they once were exactly that.

21

When the situation is this way, clearly the most wealthy and powerful need to come down to the level of their adversary and COMPROMISE.

Otherwise the end result would be genocide or annihilation.

The Iranians are too proud to discuss these things openly, as they also bray from roof tops about the great Persian Empire etc, but the reality is that their pride is similar to the Japanese in World War 2, who were finally ended and humiliated with 2 massive nuclear blasts in Nagasaki and Hiroshima.

The fact remains that the combined wealth and GDP of Iran's mortal enemies, named above (Saudi Arabia 700.1 billion USD (2020), Israel (402 billion USD (2020)), Great Britain (2.708 trillion USD (2020)), United States (20.94 trillion USD (2020)) and the rest of the allies against Iran dwarves its 191.7 billion USD (2020).

It is thus easy to conclude that the biggest baddest bullies on the block need to come down from their perch and listen to the demands of Iran, for humanity's sake.

Merely puffing and blowing up Iran to be some type of worthy financial and military adversary is completely and totally ridiculous, and is also shameful, at that.

As stated above, America's Founding Fathers probably would not have approved of the United States becoming an international bully on the world stage, acting much like the pompous European monarchies that they escaped from for their own Independence starting in the 1500s.

In fact, the Founding Fathers probably would have cheered on and applauded the naked courage and stamina of the Iranians rather than the international bullies calling for their existential destruction (or replacement of leadership).

Just like the USA supported the Afghanistan resistance against the Communist Soviet Union in the 1970s and 1980s (under Reagan and Zbigniew Brzezinski no less).

After all, the Iranians are short on money, but long on heart and soul.

Kind of like Rocky Balboa in all of the movie series.

The Communist Chinese, long bullied and discriminated against by the same hitherto named international colonialist bullies, recognized this, and therefore awarded Iran with a $400 billion trade deal over 25 years as a big middle finger to the colonialist pricks described above.

True to fact, Iran has legitimate gripes and grievances, and the powers that be should listen to them, and change their ways, rather than the other way around.

Disagreement and debate is good, unilateral exercise of power in a unipolar world, is never good.

Enter the Russian Federation, who is also doing its best to maintain the international balance of power along with Communist China.

They all have something to teach the global powers, including NATO.

Compromise is always the best option, because fighting to the death rarely solves the innate problems which force countries to physically fight one another (unless one factors in the Military Industrial Complex which always loves to supply the military hardware for a good, long fight and slog lasting many years in as many countries, for a profit, of course).

Once again, undersigned author begs the question as to why the world can not simply lock these warring sanctioning powers into a proverbial room, where they are forced to come to another peace agreement, lasting another 100 years or so.

At least, as Bono of U2 once said, "I believe in the kingdom come, when all the colors will bleed into one."

CHAPTER 8

Even Left-Wing Democrats, When They Are In Power, Can't Do Anything About Big Tech, Big Banks, Big Insurance, and Big Real Estate

For all of their hemming and hawing, spewing vitriol at conservatives and Republicans for "hoarding all of the country's wealth, the Democrats are no better, and might be worse, than their opposition for political power against the above referenced out of control, monopoly (see cartel), antitrust violating American industries which threaten the freedom, liberty and constitutional rights of every American citizen.

In fact, leftist (sometimes openly socialist as in the case of current U.S. Senator Bernie Sanders) are given a wholesale "pass" by the entire country because their very presence is synonymous with breaking up and dismantling out of control behemoth financial entities seemingly non-responsive to the people.

But the reality is far more sinister - these monstrous enemies seem to do better during these left-wing regimes (currently in power under President Biden *et al*) because they jive well and sinuously meld into the leftist world view of communism and socialism, whereby it's just a hop, jump, and a skip away from private corporate giants, to state controlled giants, with a simple stroke of the executive or legislative pen, and where they would probably do the exact same things that they are doing now to quell and crush rebellion, and the peoples' freedom in almost every capacity as guaranteed by the Bill of Rights, all in the name of the STATE.

So maybe that's why the current variety of Antitrust enforcement leaders such as Lina Khan of the Federal Trade Commission, and Jonathan Kanter of the United States Department of Justice, have done absolutely nothing to bring down the 4 antitrust elephants of the apocalypse listed above.

Similarly, left wing judges, both federal and state, do everything within their power to drag out these cases, some of which were painfully and with great difficulty initiated during the last Republican conservative administration under former Attorney General Bill Barr, and are also achieving nothing but massive billable hours generated on both sides by their lawyers, with these private corporate behemoths paying out of their nose quite easily (a drop in the bucket out of their annual monstrous trillion dollar profits) to private mega law firms, or the federal government paying off the U.S. and District Attorneys (and states attorneys general) stolen from the poor hapless taxpayers that are ironically the original victims of all of this.

It's time to hold all leaders, regardless of political persuasion or party, responsible and place their proverbial feet to the fire and bring down these massive 4 financial industries, rather than have them merge with the United States government as they are already doing now (the very definition of fascism), before finally devolving into governmental socialism, followed then by true blue communism, until we are left, by natural inertia, into the bowels of one world, one leader Luciferian dictatorship.

We are in the end game, now.

CHAPTER 9

The Incredible Short-Sightedness (And Stupidity) of the European Union Global Media Censors

The planners of Central Global media are either really stupid, or crazy like a fox.

By openly and blatantly banning any and all media tending to spew the Russian Federation's viewpoints in terms of the news, they have succeeded in only 2 things:

(1) revealing their names, identities and hand in global media affairs control (a truly evil position to have) and

(2) only delayed this "biased news" for a few hours at best, because all of those banned media outlets (RT.com, Duran, Sputnik *et al*) each have Twitter accounts, their own website pages, sister sites, private fan loyalists who spread their news with even more gusto now that they are "rebels without a case," and other leaks made even more gushing by the sheer short sightedness and stupidity of these aforementioned global media centralized planners located within the European Union, United Kingdom, and the United States of America.

In fact, it is such a massive failure in its implementation, having the exact opposite effect of making them look like the evil global empire *a la* the "Death Star," that one has to truly wonder if this was sponsored by the Russian Federation or Eurasian powers themselves.

After all, if you want to sell something like "hot cakes," first ban or limit the supply.

They could not have asked for a better Psychological Operation to bolster the Russian Federation's global support, upgrade their moral position, and otherwise augment intelligent peoples' support for their position that NATO has now criminally exceeded their mandate and has now resorted to official "international bully status."

Either way, the King Stupids and architects of this major global media debacle in banning Russian media all over the Western World, such as from "*uber* brainiac" European Commission President Ursula von der Leyen, especially considering that media freedom is protected as a fundamental right enshrined in the Universal Declaration of Human Rights and under Article 10 of the European Convention on Human Rights.

So these people are not only stupid, but they are international law breakers as well.

Another idiot, Josep Borrell, the EU's high representative for foreign affairs and security policy, appears to "gaslight" the entire world when he states "Systematic information manipulation and disinformation by the Kremlin is applied as an operational tool in its assault on Ukraine. It is also a significant and direct threat to the Union's public order and security."

Just substitute the world "Kremlin" for "NATO" and the nation "Ukraine" for "Russian Federation" (or Donbass) and you immediately get the flavor of the outcome-determinative horseshit being shoveled by these EU imbecile fascists.

Other EU dolts include Commission Vice President for Values and Transparency Věra Jourová and Internal Market Commissioner Thierry Breton, and French Digital Secretary of State Cédric O.

So while we know who some of these "leaders" (read - straw men) are, we really need to find the massive monetary sources who placed these cretins into power, in the first place.

But that is a subject for another article, possibly fueled by such luminary investigative journalists as Glenn Greenwald, Abby Martin, Caleb Maupin, or Whitney Webb.

Indeed, **_THE_** cornerstone and most important law in the United States of America is the First Amendment, i.e., freedom of speech and expression, which was struck by the nation's Founding Fathers as the first law of the land in response to the thousands years long and draconian civil and human rights violations, oppressions, taking without paying, and tyrannical behavior of Europe's most cruel and sadistic oligarchs, plutocrats and monarchs, as they set out to establish a new world in the Americas.

And this is why true blue, red blooded Americans are at the very least, uncomfortable with the EU's behavior.

The only ones dragging the USA along for the ride are those corrupted senators, congressman, executive and judicial members who are "on the take" somehow on this global plutocrat money, benefits, sweetheart real estate deals and mortgages, outright bribery, corruption or cronyism, for them or their family and friends.

Certainly not real Americans who understand the United States Constitution, men like Kentucky U.S. Senator Rand Paul, who sometimes seems to be the only bulwark in the U.S. Government able to resist the obscene amounts of money and power being thrown at these government clowns like rice at a wedding.

CHAPTER 10

The Extreme Speed By Which The Western World Closed Off Russia Proves That The "Conspiracy Theorists" Were Correct

It is extremely difficult to shut down all aspects and facets of a person's life, let alone a small business or company.

But to shut down an entire nation in almost every regard is nothing short of miraculous, if unprecedented.

Not only did the unified Western powers, including but not limited to the European Union and the United States shut down, within a matter of hours/days, Russia's diplomatic relations after their invasion of Ukraine in February 2022, but they also successfully shut down their:

(1)   global media propagation;

(2)   global internet access;

(3)   access to global banking system and SWIFT;

(4)   confiscated their real and non-tangible global property and assets;

(5)   defamed and ruined their global reputation;

(6)   got global internet media conglomerates such as Google, FaceBook (Meta) and even China's Tik Tok to disavow Russian Television and Sputnik;

(7)   expelled their Diplomats;

(8)   sanctioned their MVP billionaire oligarchs even if they did not agree with the Ukraine invasion;

(9)   closed down their money transmission and merchant accounts;

(10) cut off their food/medicine supply and ability to export; and

much, much more.

For decades now, and picking up speed in the last few years, various "conspiracy theorists" have sworn that there were only a few individuals powerful and connected enough to shut down all or some of the above referenced aspects of human existence, but they were roundly and soundly scoffed at, as being paranoid. No one is laughing anymore.

CHAPTER 11

Trouble Ahead: Major Banks and Merchant Services Merging Into One

In what could be the storyline for an A-level conspiracy theory blockbuster movie by Hollywood's best producers/directors, it appears that the leaders of both the Federal Trade Commission and U.S. Department of Justice Antitrust Divisions, who have been asleep at the wheel for decades straight, have begun to yield fruit.

Major banks and more egregiously, merchant services companies (i.e., credit card acceptance entities) have been merging rapidly and quietly to the point that the whenever one is charging a credit card, it goes through any one of the top-most companies that are either the same company using a different name, or have recently merged, or simply are branches/affiliates/subsidiaries of one another.

Case in point is FIS, which could also be FISERV, which also could be World Pay, which also could be accessmyiq.com, and more.

A simple scan of each of these companies Better Business Bureau listings show that they are apparently "separate entities," but if one files a complaint with either the Consumer Financial Protection Bureau ("CFPB"), the New York State Department of Financial Services, the Better Business Bureau ("BBB"), the Office of the Comptroller of the Currency ("OCC"), the Federal Reserve, or even the Federal Deposit Insurance Corporation ("FDIC"), one inevitably gets the typical "kiss off letter," cc'ing all of these "investigative agencies" in open and brazen disrespect, arrogance and haughtiness, from one or more of these agencies, even if you filed a complaint against a differently named one.

What does this mean for banking consumers, whether individual or small business?

It means that, just like in one of the "Terminator" movies, when you poke or stroke one part of this "liquid metallic-like" entity with a complaint for illegal or unethical banking activity, your complaint gets absorbed/sucked in, while another part of this vast goopy entity strikes back at you with a canned response essentially saying, "wasn't me!"

This style of doing business by major banks and their major merchant services companies serves many functions, all to the benefit of them, while screwing the common man:

(1) evades responsibility; (2) confuses customers; (3) confuses regulatory agencies; (4) shifts responsibility; (5) muddles accountability; (6) centralizes banking/merchant services authority/power to some nameless/faceless entity or individual; (7) establishes plausible denial of actual fault or blame; and (8) helps them to avoid prosecution by antitrust law enforcement.

Humanity is currently in a dire situation, where constant news headlines include topics such as "banks close account based on the target's politics," or "merchant services refuse to do business with an entity because of their public statements," or "targeted individual or business or entity has their duly earned money held up for 6 months due to investigation," and other scary headlines which cover up one basic fact - that these obscenely huge financial behemoths are literally depriving their customers (or more appropriately their "subjects") of their life, liberty, and property because they have expressed themselves consistent with the First Amendment of the United States Constitution, and are now being handily punished for the same.

All the while, the People (and their bought off and paid for legislators in the congress and senate, including their "Banking Committees") are asleep at the wheel, or have no idea that this is happening.

The Congressional and Senate Banking Committees obviously now that this is occurring, but the essential and inherent flaw in United States government elections being the "lobbying" and "political contributions" getting people into office, made infinitely worse by such satanic case law as Justice John Roberts sanctioned "Citizens United" case, which allowed multi-national, multi-billion dollar companies, with no loyalty to any national borders or laws, only to their own multi-national profits, ultimately vitiate and undermine the United States Constitution to replace it with "international arbitration agreements," succeeded in overthrowing the United States and replacing its leadership and three branches of government, without even firing a single shot.

Gone are the wars of conquest, the last one being the War Of 1812, where British bankers using cannon-fodder British troops attacked and burned down their upstart American cousins' towns, cities, businesses, property, and people for daring to speak their minds and rebel against their European banking oppressors.

The establishment of the Federal Reserve centralized (and privately owned) bank and the institution of the federal income tax both in 1913 quickly put an end to those freedoms guaranteed by the United States Constitution.

Any enemies of this foreign banker invasion and their domestic policies into the United States were quickly smacked down by the also newly formed from the constitutional Bureau of Investigation formed in 1908 but then transformed into the unconstitutional, Freemasonic Federal Bureau of Investigation ("FBI") headed up by fellow Freemasonic Shriner, J. Edgar Hoover, and any challenges to their foreign policies were met head on by the also newly formed Central Intelligence Agency ("CIA"), which was helped along into unconstitutional development from the constitutional Office of Strategic Services ("OSS") by the thoroughly Freemasonic British Intelligence Services, MI-6 and MI-5.

This problem was highlighted recently, when Federal Reserve Chief Janet Yellen went on public television in front of the U.S. Congress and Senate and essentially declared that abortion should be legalized because it was good for the economy in eliminating "useless eaters" as coined by Henry Kissinger in his National Security Memo NSSM 200.

The last person who echoed these sentiments was the founder of Planned Parenthood, Margaret Sanger, whose eugenics and racist views on human life formed the inspiration for Adolph Hitler's race-based eugenics laws that paved the way for the NAZI Holocaust.

CHAPTER 12

Unfortunately, Organized Jewry Are Also Organized Bullies

It pains the undersigned author to write the above title for this Op-Ed article, but sadly after 50 years of observation of International Organized Jewry, from childhood all the way to well educated and successful adult international lawyer having his own 21 year old law practice on Wall Street, and all of the experiences in between, many of which have been documented in this Deep State Defector series I through IV, undersigned author rarely makes a statement that he can not back up with cold, objective, and hard fact.

This may be due to the rigorous training and CEO as a lawyer in one of the roughest and toughest cities to make it in the world, Manhattan, New York City.

And in no small measure, undersigned's ethnic heritage, hailing from the Arya Samaj "reform movement" of Hinduism, established, spearheaded, and pioneered by legendary Freemasons and Luciferians Madam Helena Blavatsky, Swami Dayananda Saraswati, Swami Vivekananda, Annie Besant, and other restless Luciferians looking to save the world with illumination and light, some would call it "Tikkun Olam," may have had something to do with this conclusion, as well.

For if undersigned is not distinctly born into an arcane far flung sect of crypto-Judaism in the great tradition of the Donmeh Muslims of

37

Turkey under Rabbi Shabtai Zvi, or Basque crypto-Jew "Saint" Ignatius Loyola and his brand of crypto-Jewry conversos marano Catholics, whom he organized into the Jesuits of the International Society of Jesus, or maybe even the other sects of Judaism descended from the steppes of the Khazarian grasslands under Kagan (King) Bulent who *en masse* converted his predominantly pagan Baal/Moloch followers to Judaism from pagan tengrism, having more in common with Ghengis Khan than Jesus Christ and the ancient middle eastern Israelities, than nothing ever could.

But the fact remains that the reason that so many religious Hasidic Jews, such as Rabbi Dovid Weiss of his Neturei Karta sect, who choose to interpret the literal meaning contained within their holy books Torah and Talmud are horrified by the Israeli Jews who impatiently decided to "become their own Messiah" by forging with blood, cash, murder, bullying, apartheid, "by way of deception to do war," tons of cold hard cash, insidious lobbying power, if not pure extortion of governments and oligarchs exercised by such men as Jeffrey Epstein, the Black Cube, Mossad, and all of their proxies in between in nearly all of the governments of the world, this should come as no surprise, because they really were not supposed to do that.

Instead they should have waited until the Moschiach arrived in due course and due time, not squeezed through Luciferian rose colored glasses by men, chanting "Never Again" and more suited to be serial killers and butchers than statesmen or "men of God."

Even Albert Einstein called these men such as Israeli leader Menachem Begin, "fascists" and "terrorists."

It seems that there was no limit on the price that these "founding fathers of Israel" would pay for these delusional Luciferian impatient Jewish "men of God" to forge a new nation with their own hands, bodies, brains, and to use those of others who never had a choice in the matter.

How many innocent souls have died in this quest to forge a new Israel, to build the Third Temple, the Knesset, and other Israeli institutional and edifice recreations hailing back to King Solomon, is no mean feat of calculation, but it has been estimated to be around a total of 24,068 IDF soldiers, police officers, prison wardens, Shin Bet security service and Mossad agents have been killed defending the land of Israel since 1860, the year that the first Jewish settlers left the secure walls of Jerusalem to build new neighborhoods.[1]

And this was just the Jews that were killed, and does not take into account all of the hundreds of millions of innocent people all around the world who have been killed in Israeli originated and lobbied for proxy wars waged by powerful nation states on behalf of the octopus-like International Israeli lobby, which sits in nearly every major country known today, pulling the strings of their host governments, all under the anonymous and amorphous guise of the "Deep State," as was coined by legendary CIA Chief of Staff Philip Giraldi to describe the formerly Jewish but now Muslim converted Donmeh of Turkey.

Those former Jews who converted to Islam to please the Ottoman Sultan in 1666, but like the Catholic conversos from Judaism, refused to accept the religion and instead destroyed them from within by advancing "secularism," in the form of Mustafa Kemal Ataturk, also a Donmeh and Freemason.

Let's see if their efforts will yield fruit in the production of this much anticipated Moshiach.

---

[1] Sources: Israel Ministry of Foreign Affairs; Israel Government Press Office; IDF; Haaretz, (April 19, 2015); "IDF: 56 soldiers died since last Memorial Day, bringing total to 23,741," Times of Israel, (May 3, 2019).
"Israel comes to a standstill to remember 23,928 fallen," Times of Israel, (April 13, 2021). Anna Ahronheim, "56 IDF soldiers and security personnel died in 2021 - Defense Ministry," Jerusalem Post, (April 29, 2022).

CHAPTER 13

The Oligarch/Communist/ Plutocrat Trend Towards Insurance Companies Denying Claims

In previous articles, undersigned author has written extensively about how the global oligarchs have now merged with the global communists, in order to exert a hitherto unprecedented stranglehold on the world's people under one system of government.

Whereas it used to be, big business and tycoons fighting against the government to exert their own freedoms, now it has emerged that the *uber* wealthy have realized that it is much better to own, or merge with the government, than to fight against it.

This is of course only a natural occurrence after the last few decades wherein the masses around the world protested against being the 99%, while the 1% seemed to own every elected leader, politician, judge, legislator, law enforcement agency, and all of the NGOs in between.

Those protestors distinctly smelled blood in the water, and tried to warn the world with their global protests and Guy Fawkes masks.

But the battle is coming to an end, and the leaders in government are now unabashedly defying the needs of their governed people while catering to their donor (briber) oligarchs and plutocrats.

Nowhere is this more apparent than in the Insurance Industry, wherein even well-heeled, wealthy small business, corporations, and budding CEOs are getting routinely denied on their legitimate claims for liability insurance, even if they pay through the nose in exorbitant premium costs, never miss a payment, and sign up honestly for coverage in case they are attacked.

But even the Senate and Congressional committees that regulate and monitor the insurance industry, such as famously incompetent Pat Toomey, let alone the multiple state agencies such as New York's incompetent and lethargic Department of Financial Services, seem to buy, hook, line and sinker, any and all lame and illegitimate claim denials submitted by even the dumbest of insurance company claims adjustors and analysts, from almost all of the big insurance companies in the world.

It is comical to see that almost each and every claim or lawsuit has a "disclaimer" specifically touching on that specifically raised issue, or is stretched to the limit of reason on each one, just so that these corrupted government employees can, out of hand and summarily, dismiss the inevitable complaints that necessarily follow from their wrongfully denied insureds.

The insurance industry has become a modern day snakeoil salesmen business, promising their hapless gullible customers that "nationwide is on your side" but then meanwhile anally raping them when it comes time to cover their insureds against bona fide, legitimate, obviously covered claims.

But who will rescue the people when their own government regulators are in bed with the oligarchs/plutocrats that own these insurance companies?

Rinse, lather and repeat the above, only substitute "insurance industry" with "big tech,' and now you will see the trend, even clearer.

This is happening in virtually every big industry in America, and consequently, the world.

CHAPTER 14

TikTok And HuaWei: The U.S. Government Is The King Of Projection, Gaslighting And Hypocrisy

The overwhelming hypocrisy, gaslighting, and projection of the United States government of its own bad acts when it comes to foreign countries, leaders, cultures and even people should never cease to amaze the average world citizen, especially Americans.

While out of control American Big Tech buys and sells our elected leaders and politicians in all 3 branches of government like farm animals in order to do their bidding under the color of governmental law and authority, in total violation of 42 U.S.C. § 1983, when they are discovered and found out about, they instantly resort to name calling and the general *chutzpah* of claiming that the "others" are doing what they are doing, only it's better that they are doing it, because they are "American companies."

In point of fact, a glaring example of this is how American Big Tech, threatened by technology coming out of the east, i.e., China, in the form of TikTok, or HuaWei, are declaring that there are somehow "national security threats" because "their technology is stealing bio-data, identifying personal information, images, likenesses, and other information" which could likely "invade the privacy of ordinary Americans, and our children."

Children.

43

They always throw that word in, because, like the Hitler-coined phrase, "best interests of the children" that gets red blooded Americans fired up, guaranteed.

But the U.S. Government, based on its own track record, at least for the last 75 years since World War II, after British Intelligence and German NAZI scientists transformed (see, infected) the once singularly patriotic military intelligence agency, the Office of Strategic Services ("OSS") into today's Central Intelligence Agency ("CIA"), is no one to judge the good (or bad) intentions of any other nation or foreign entity's relative harm or foul to the American or global population.

So while American Big tech steals all of that same information and data from the world's people and also uses it for their own nefarious purposes, it inures to the benefit of their corrupt and satanic oligarchs and plutocrats, corrupt politicians and elected leaders, and other undesirables who don't give a rat's ass about the general welfare of the public, or the American people in general.

But last I heard, the Peoples Republic of China actually (in contrast to the United States) routinely takes corrupt politicians and business leaders (oligarchs) "to the woodshed" and punishes them openly and harshly, if they ever engage in behavior tending to corrupt or harm the people that they govern, as a "breach of the public trust."

Recently, China's equivalent to Jeff Bezos of Amazon, CEO Jack Ma of "Ali Baba," disappeared inexplicably for a very long time until it was released that he may have engaged in activity unbecoming of an oligarch, while also recently Hu Jin Tao, former premier of China, was recently led away from a public dinner honoring current prime minister Xi Jinping, also for corruption reasons allegedly.

But here in America, we give guys like Henry Paulson, former magnate and head of Goldman Sachs who single handedly tanked the United States economy in 2008 by spearheading the mortgage banking crisis, instead of incarceration, he was given the job of Secretary of the U.S. Treasury by dim-witted former President George W Bush and equally evil Vice President Dick Cheney.

I don't know about you, but I would rather have my personal information, if the government is going to steal it anyway and inevitably, to be in the hands of a nation that legally and equitably crucifies corrupt and dishonest politicians and its oligarchs/plutocrats, rather than offering them pivotal jobs and responsibilities within the government itself.

Let's face it, those guys are not going to get more honest when they assume a government title as when they were working in the private sector (which seems to be the revolving door norm in American society).

The United States seems to rewards its scoundrels, thieves, robbers, scam artists, monopolists, and major criminals with government roles rather than throwing them into a hole for the rest of their lives, while China, does not.

They do just the opposite, as a breach of the public good.

And again, while undersigned author is NO FAN of communism or socialism, having written countless articles opposing being controlled by scurrilous people hiding within and behind the US government, perhaps the first step in learning to live with the seemingly inevitable future of more government control and intrusion into our lives, is to also entertain a ZERO TOLERANCE POLICY for those government officials who even have one whisker dipped into the trough of public corruption and criminality.

CHAPTER 15

Those Who Opposed Unchecked Migration Must Communicate With Those Country's Leaders

Right now, the United States of America is being torn apart politically by the monied forces that want unbridled unlimited migration into the USA from foreign countries, most notably epitomized by the multi-billionaire George Soros, and opposed by the equally monied interests that are militantly against it.

However just like in every country, the only way for countries to curb and control their incoming flux of migrants into their own countries is to have sustained and productive dialogue with the leadership of those nations sending those migrants in.

This "leadership" includes not only government workers and executives, but also private sector oligarchs and private business owners, as no amount of sustained uncontrolled illegal migration into the USA (or any country) could exist without the full acquiescence if not total control of this illicit process by that nation's ruling class.

In many ways, the situation mirrors the Mariel Crisis in the 1980s where Fidel Castro apparently emptied his own jails and shipped some of his hardest criminals into the United States, with many arguing that this was somehow a form of asymmetric warfare designed to infuse the United

States with mentally ill and dangerous criminals in order to depress the US economy and endanger the safety and national security of the United States.

Similarly today, many are arguing that the simultaneous busloads and caravans of illegal migrants, coupled with massive amounts of the extremely deadly fentanyl drug being intermixed with powdered cocaine, crystal meth, and other forms of illicit narcotics are fueling and strengthening the South American drug trade by supplying both much-needed foot labor for the 5 major Mexican drug cartels, but also working together with Communist China and remnants of Islamic Terrorist groups, a method with which to kill and target young Americans and weaken the resolve and collective mood of the United States.

These methods of asymmetric warfare are more psychological weapons than catastrophic weapons of mass destruction, but their corresponding deleterious effects on the US economy and national security are almost identical.

Those Americans (especially the wealthy ones) should begin to open up dialogues with foreign leadership (both public and private, but without violating the Logan Act) in order to stem, curb, and control the tide of this illegal method of asymmetric warfare.

If this can not be accomplished, then those Americans should pressure their elected representatives in the United States Congress, Senate, and Executive branches to do so.

Chapter 16

Communism Capitalizes On Extremism

In order for organized communism to exert its will on the people that it governs, it must be able to justify its mass curtailment of individual human rights, civil liberties and police state power over the most minute areas of each of its citizens daily lives.

The abusive use of "terrorism" to justify this expansive state police power is the most important aspect of this justification, and so the communist state takes great exertion to either fight, or even to create, "extremist" elements within its society.

Critical to this is the mass categorization of its people, and to bolster, create or even encourage various extremist sectors within those categories.

This is also known as "salami tactics," as previously described by the author.

In the United States, extremist groups are used to crush or quell legitimate aspirations of the citizenry for their inalienable civil rights as guaranteed by the United States Constitution and the Bill of Rights.

The super wealthy oligarchs, otherwise known as plutocrats, enjoy their stranglehold on the American domestic and foreign economy, policy, and culture, and generally view the struggle for equality or fight for civil rights by its crushed and oppressed masses as threats to that stranglehold.

This is why the Federal Bureau of Investigation ("FBI") and the Central Intelligence Agency ("CIA"), for example, fight to crush these aspirations by their governed people on behalf of the oligarchs and plutocrats, using "extremism" and "terrorism" as their excuse.

And this is another reason why, time and time again, both the FBI and the CIA have been caught red-handed in either instigating, creating, fomenting, and willingly participating in elaborate extremist and terrorist arrests, indictments, charges, convictions, and recommendations to the executive and legislature to pass sweeping, unconstitutional, and oppressive federal and state laws designed to gut the U.S. Constitution and the ability of the people to obtain redress for their civil rights deprivations under the color of law and authority, as described in 42 USC § 1983.

In fact, entire cottage industries have been set up within the various U.S. Attorneys Offices as administered under the U.S. Department of Justice using established oppressive and draconian case law to instantly quash and crush any attempt for potential civil rights litigants to obtain redress in the courts.

Some of these cases include Younger v Harris, Bevins, DeShaney vs. Winnebago, and Town of Castle Rock vs. Gonzales for example, whereby over and over the federal courts dismiss and sometimes even sanction or place into jail those courageous few who gather the courage and ability to sue their oppressors in the courts.

Couples with Anti-SLAPP legislation, the climb uphill towards civil rights vindication becomes even more dangerous as any lawyer who attempts to fight for their client's civil rights faces contempt, suspension, disbarment, or even jail time depending upon the whim of the presiding judge or magistrate hearing the case, these judges and magistrates 99% of the time having been placed there in the first place by the wealthy oppressive oligarchs and plutocrats, in the first place (see lobbying power, or legalized bribery).

This vicious circle unfortunately is the rule in American jurisprudence, and is becoming worse, year after year, decade after decade, as the wealthy become wealthier, the middle class erodes more and more to be replaced by a growing underclass and poverty stricken society, and the antitrust divisions of both the U.S. Department of Justice and the Federal Trade Commission continue to ignore their responsibilities and allow companies and the oligarchs running them to continue to merge, consolidate, and buy one another out so that they become too difficult for the executive and legislative and judicial branches to control, reel in, regulate, pare down, or punish for various criminal and civil offenses against the American (and global) people.

This is particularly troublesome as currently, renegade loudmouth senators and congressmen such as Senators Bernie Sanders and Elizabeth Warren, who have made a career out of yelling about "bringing down the billionaires" and "helping the common man" can (and will) do nothing to fulfil their campaign promises and rhetoric, even now, while they are currently in power during the present Biden Administration.

The phrase, "goodbye to the old boss, say hello to the new boss" has no better meaning than the current state of affairs wherein very little has changed in terms of domestic or foreign policy from either this current administration, and prior administrations, whether "republican" or "democrat," "liberal" or "conservative."

And just like in the former Soviet Union, this speeding, out of control freight train, will only be stopped when the country eventually ruptures and explodes, by the now swollen oligarch ticks who have gorged on the peoples' metaphorical blood and wealth more and more, unimpeded and uninhibited by the US Government, year after year.

To use another analogy, the country will continue to progress down this path until the oligarch viruses, which have infected their host cell America, break open and kill their host when they can no longer suck any more of their wealth and rights and prosperity away from the People.

CHAPTER 17

The United States Government Use Of Out Of Control Oligarchs And Countries To Break The Law

For the past 70 years, the United States of America government, in all three branches (executive, legislative, and judiciary) have made good use of the proxy world in accomplishing not only their legal goals, but also, with great and alarming ever increasing frequency, their illegal, immoral, and criminal goals, all in violation of the worlds' and its own federal, state and local law.

For example, the US Government promulgates laws that forbid murder and assassination - so instead the US intelligence services and military makes use of various rogue nations throughout the world as veritable "hit men" to take out their enemies, either open or clandestine.

Favorite choices are using Israel, Saudi Arabia, and other countries where lawlessness is heavily intertwined with how much money exchanges hands by and between the USA and that nation.

Additionally, everyone knows that the United States has a U.S. Constitution, with the first and most important Amendment being, just that, the First Amendment, which guarantees the right to free and open expression of speech and communication without hindrance, harassment, obstruction, or financial retaliation or punishment by said US Government.

However, enter the world of Big Technology, comprised of such morally upstanding (sarcasm) tech trillionaire (sarcasm) "private corporation" giants as Google, Yelp, Bing Microsoft, FaceBook, Amazon, Twitter, and other gargantuan behemoths that literally have woven a web around the United States of America and its citizenry, as well as around the rest of the world, to stifle, muffle, shut down, "cancel," drown out, silence and retaliate against anyone and everyone who speaks out against the foreign and domestic policies that only a few 100 American oligarchs possess and get passed, through their direct prostitutes in the U.S. Congress and Senate, through "election donations" and other such legalized bribery and public corruption.

These Big Tech empires are immune from lawsuits by the Communications Decency Act § 230 while they curtail, control, stifle and muffle free speech, literature, news, free expression, and free thought with impunity while having more money and power than the United States government.

Then of course enter the Big Banks/Finance, which effectively have the ability to shut down anyone and everyone financially if they "step out of line" in any way, thus forcing that targeted individual or business to struggle to buy and sell, pay bills or rent, or even eat, thus starving them into submission, all in violation of ethics and morality, but apparently not the law, since they are also "private corporations" not engaging in "state action" regulated by the United States Constitution.

The United State Supreme Court case, Citizens United v FEC solidified this mass financial rape of U.S. Democracy and the Constitutional Bill of Rights by allowing billionaire oligarchs, like the late and former casino boss Sheldon Adelson, to be the only singular voice controlling former President Trump through his agents National Security tools John Bolton, Mike Pompeo, Brian Hook, and other mercenary souls to bomb Iran, and thus start World War III, at the behest of Israel and other aggressive Zionist Jews throughout the world.

And this mechanism is not just limited to the right, or the left.

The left wing has billionaire oligarch titans like George Soros pushing a veritable communist agenda, while the right wing Oligarchs have heavy hitters such as Elon Musk, Peter Thiel, Paul Singer, Robert Mercer, Stephen Schwarzman, the Koch family, and others pulling the political puppet strings in the U.S., throwing American into veritable left-wing communism and then into near capitalist right-wing oligarchical feudalism, with every successive presidential and legislator election every few years.

Chapter 18

The U.S. Government Plausible Denial Trend Using Big Tech Proxies Only Gets Bigger

If you haven't been sleeping under a rock for the past decade or so, you will notice that the United States Government (all 3 branches, judicial, legislative and executive) have not only done nothing meaningful in terms of taking down or dismantling the ever-growing and ever more dangerous monopoly/cartel/antitrust-violating Big Tech monsters coming out of the West Coast, but have actually wilfully contributed to their growth and out of control exacerbation.

This is precisely because, like the great old tradition of the U.S. Government using proxy nations, countries, paramilitary organizations, even the Mafia, they have discovered that they can try and remain faithful and true to the United States Constitution if they themselves can establish "plausible denial" that they had anything to do with the myriad and countless federal, state and local crimes being committed by Big Tech under their watch.

For example, because the vast majority of Big Tech consists of "private corporations," the Federal Trade Commission and the U.S. Department of Justice Anti-Trust Division are able to disavow or ignore when, for example, Amazon.com, the biggest purveyor of online and physical books, media and television, openly censor a massive amount of information if they do not tow the line of their terms of service, thus completely undermining and destroying the First Amendment pertaining to freedom of speech and expression of ideas.

Similarly, when FaceBook (now known as "Meta,") buys and sells the most personal and sensitive bio-data and private information of their users (including biometrics) to the highest bidder, many of whom have insidious and harmful goals in mind, no one in the U.S. Government (including judges) bat an eyelash because of the protections of the Communications Decency Act § 230 ("CDA 230"), which effectively bans any and all lawsuits and liability against internet service providers or website owners/hosts thereon, drafted by such short-sighted if not evil Senators Ron Wyden and Chris Cox.

Taking this spear into the side of the American people (and the world), these same bought off and bribed (see "lobbied") government employees in all three branches of the U.S. Government have also allowed Google, arguably the worst offender of them all in Big Tech, to break nearly every federal, state and local law known to mankind, as well as direct head on collisions with the United States Constitution involving the 1st, 2nd, 4th, 5th, 6th Amendments, if not the entire United States Bill of Rights.

But again, Google leaders such as Eric Schmidt, Larry Page, Jared Cohen, and Sergey Brin have intermingled so much of the U.S. intelligence and national security apparatus, if not the entire military industrial complex, that it is impossible to know the difference.

But they have been able to dodge any accountability because of their deep pockets, outright bribery of countless members of the U.S. Government (see again - "lobbying power") that not even presiding federal judges can know their ass from their elbow about where the government begins, and where Google finishes the criminal tasks off.

This is again, known as "plausible denial," and is a principal as old as the Central Intelligence Agency itself, also on par with the "black bag jobs" of the Federal Bureau of Investigation, which were both called to the mat and banned during the Frank Church senate hearings of 1976.

At least its predecessor, the Office of Strategic Services (aka "OSS") had some integrity when they were led and staffed by such war heroes as "Wild Bill" Donovan and other American heroes.

But after World War II, and after the infection and subsequent transformation of the OSS by imported British intelligence and NAZI Germany scientists during Operation Paperclip to form the CIA, America (and Big Tech) has never been the same.

Chapter 19

Why Man Needs God At This Moment In Time

Charles Bukowski once said, "The problem with the world is that the intelligent people are full of doubts, while the stupid ones are full of confidence."

This eloquently summarizes the plight of modern man, today, on planet earth, rapidly moving towards a one world order, whether one likes it, or not.

The problem is that a few elite "thought leaders" have emerged on the global stage, blessed by the limited idiots at universities such as Harvard, Yale, Stanford, Oxford, Cambridge and the like, professing to be literal "Gods on Earth," blessed with the innate ability to rule over man and animal alike, in the absence of the God head.

These university-sanctioned imbeciles have now been joined by the troglodyte trillionnaires of extreme internet Big Tech finance, those "Geeks of yesterday" who have now blown up into the "megalomaniacs of today," with equal parts Napoleonic-complex and Christ-like messiah complex, who also fashion themselves into veritable "God-men."

Add to this viscous unhealthy soup of malignant egos, is the secret society of Freemasonry, which has been infiltrated by more sociopathic people, religions, extremists, and society's refuse than one cares to imagine, who espouse as their motto *"Deus Meumque Jus,"* which, literally translates to "God, Residing Within Me" (see, *Luciferianism*).

These sociopathic secret society idiots therefore lend an air of religious credibility to these aggressive arrogant psychopaths, who are then convinced, through sheer multi-generational peer pressure and overwhelming repetition, that they are somehow the planet's "betters," and should therefore take the place of the Ultimate, or "God," as he has most assuredly abandoned his creation, if he ever existed at all (*"Deism"*).

Unfortunately, it is very difficult for these "chosen people" to see through and navigate through all of these various levels of wool being pulled before their eyes (see "bullshit") and therefore have a great deal of difficulty seeing clearly, or even thinking with lucidity.

And unfortunately, these are the men (and women) who run our world and meet at these Bilderberg Conferences, where they chart and plan the world's events, one by one, piece by piece, component by component, and dare we say, false flag after false flag (see *Operation Gladio*, for example).

It is vitally important for the worlds' leaders to have a healthy dose of "humility," if they wish to assume the mantle of global leadership, and always questioning their daily decisions, big or small, so as to minimize the chances that humanity and all that is living on planet earth fall into the chasm of global destruction and abyss.

Indeed, the ruins of the past, some scientists dating them as far back as hundreds of thousands of years old, such as the awe-inspiring Pyramids of Giza, or the human head statutes at Easter Island, harken to a time when men also reached towards the skies of human and mental development, but were somehow quickly, abruptly, and without warning, blighted out of existence (could that have been irresponsible nuclear cataclysm, as we are also so close to, today)?

Only humility in our leaders should be the main requirement, as also self-doubt, in that every leadership step should be taken in consult with countless others, after great thought, deliberation, and rumination, and not the "A to Z" tyrannical approach of most of our impatient world leaders, today.

Only then can we artificially extend our short lifespan on this planet, one generation after the next, in this day and age, when we are all sitting atop the fuse of the greatest bomb in history, planet earth laden with nuclear missiles and weapons of mass destruction in the tens of thousands, situated all over our planet, for maximum blast effect, placed there by our "betters."